THE WORLD'S GREATEST DAD

Written, Designed and Illustrated
by Martin Riskin

To Phil Riskin
Who inspired the concept of this book.

Published simultaneously in Canada by
Marka Canada, Toronto, Ontario

Distributed in the United Kingdom by
Azlon London LTD., London, SW11 3UP

Manufactured in the United States of America

First Printing, March 1983
Third Printing, February 1983

IVORY TOWER PUBLISHING COMPANY, INC.
125 Walnut Street, Watertown, Massachusetts 02172
Tel: (617) 923-1111   Telex: 6971455 ITAP

THE
WORLD'S GREATEST
DAD

Was and still is my greatest fan

THE
WORLD'S GREATEST
DAD

Proved to us that smoking was definitely
harmful to our health

THE
WORLD'S GREATEST
DAD

Held me tight on my first roller coaster ride

THE
WORLD'S GREATEST
DAD

Showed me the glories of nature

THE
WORLD'S GREATEST
DAD

Let me help with the driving, sometimes

THE
WORLD'S GREATEST
DAD

Gave me important jobs to do

THE WORLD'S GREATEST
DAD

Built the most fantastic sand castles

THE WORLD'S GREATEST
DAD

Built a tree house for me

THE WORLD'S GREATEST
DAD

Taught me the fine points of baseball

THE
WORLD'S GREATEST
DAD

Protected me from a terrible movie monster

THE WORLD'S GREATEST
DAD

Hugged me the hardest when I came home
from camp

THE
WORLD'S GREATEST
DAD

Took me to the circus

THE
WORLD'S GREATEST
DAD

Always practiced pacifism

THE
WORLD'S GREATEST
DAD

Was the world's greatest chauffeur

THE
WORLD'S GREATEST
DAD

Knew that there was always a time
for sentimentality

THE WORLD'S GREATEST
DAD

Was probably the bravest warrior ever

THE WORLD'S GREATEST DAD

POLLY PENQUIN MEETS THE BIRDS & THE BEES

Taught us the facts of life

THE WORLD'S GREATEST
DAD

KISS FOR
CHARITY
BOOTH

TO BENEFIT
THE HOME FOR
UNWED CATS

Taught us to be charitable

THE
WORLD'S GREATEST
DAD

Helped us build our vocabularies

THE WORLD'S GREATEST
DAD

...while illustrating the value of humility

THE WORLD'S GREATEST
DAD

Took up too much room in a pup tent

THE WORLD'S GREATEST
DAD

Knew enough not to help us with our
homework, too much

THE
WORLD'S GREATEST
DAD

Financed our ventures

THE WORLD'S GREATEST
DAD

Taught us the responsibility of earning
money
...but spared us the hardships

THE
WORLD'S GREATEST
DAD

Showed us that losing isn't all that bad

THE
WORLD'S GREATEST
DAD

Interceded with Mom in our behalf

THE WORLD'S GREATEST DAD

Saw the advantages of good nutrition

THE
WORLD'S GREATEST
DAD

Made a bad nightmare seem silly

THE
WORLD'S GREATEST
DAD

Knew enough not to give us kids
driving lessons

THE WORLD'S GREATEST
DAD

Mediated our controversies

THE WORLD'S GREATEST
DAD

Was always a good sport

THE WORLD'S GREATEST
DAD

Showed us what a great cook mother was

THE
WORLD'S GREATEST
DAD

Taught us how to plan for the future

THE WORLD'S GREATEST
DAD

Brought us great presents when we
were sick

THE
WORLD'S GREATEST
DAD

Knew the value of a Sunday afternoon nap

THE WORLD'S GREATEST DAD

Showed us the value of a dollar

THE
WORLD'S GREATEST
DAD

Took enormous risks on our behalf

THE WORLD'S GREATEST
DAD

Showed us the importance
of saving for a rainy day

THE WORLD'S GREATEST DAD

Provided good work incentives

THE
WORLD'S GREATEST
DAD

Exposed us to good literature

THE WORLD'S GREATEST
DAD

Helped out in
financial emergencies